Literature Response Forms

Grades 6-8

Written by Eleanor M. Summers
Illustrated by S&S Learning Materials

About the author:
Eleanor M. Summers is a retired elementary teacher who continues to be involved at various levels of education. She has written many useful resources to assist teachers with their Language Arts programs.

ISBN 978-1-55495-053-9
Copyright 2009
All Rights Reserved * Printed in Canada

Published in the United States by:
On the Mark Press
P.O. Box 433
Clayton, New York
13624
www.onthemarkpress.com

Published in Canada by:
S&S Learning Materials
15 Dairy Avenue
Napanee, Ontario
K7R 1M4
www.sslearning.com

At A Glance™

Learning Expectations	Vocabulary Development	Identifying Important Information	Character Analysis	Summarizing Events	Reasoning & Critical Thinking	Creativity & Design
Understanding Concepts						
• Identify familiar parts of speech: nouns, verbs, modifiers	•					
• Identify variety of sentence types: assertive, exclamation, interrogative, imperative, and explain their use	•					
• Identify figurative language such as: simile, metaphor, imagery, personification	•	•				
• Identify literacy techniques such as: foreshadowing, irony, mood, theme	•	•		•	•	•
• Use connecting phrases and clauses to retell a story		•	•	•	•	•
• Use a dictionary and thesaurus to expand vocabulary	•					
• Show awareness of the expressiveness of words	•	•	•	•	•	•
Reading Comprehension						
• Make predictions based on evidence from the text		•		•	•	•
• Identify and describe story elements		•			•	•
• Identify main idea, provide supporting details, key words		•		•	•	•
• Summarize story elements; cite supporting evidence		•		•		
• Explain how story elements relate to each other			•	•	•	
• Identify and describe character traits and cite supporting evidence			•			•
• Identify and describe similarities and differences		•	•	•		
• Identify cause and effect relationships		•		•	•	
• Use own schema to make connections between the story and personal experiences/the real world		•	•	•	•	•
• Make inference based on personal interpretation of the story			•	•	•	•
• Make judgments and draw conclusions using evidence from the story		•	•	•	•	•
• Adapt the story for presentation to retell in another way				•	•	•
• Create a media text						•
• Creative writing – sequel to the story, join the story, rewrite the ending					•	•
• Forms of writing – book reviews, book report, biography		•		•	•	•
• Express own interpretation of a story through visual and performing arts (illustrations, picture book, theatrical script)		•		•	•	•
• Develop opinions and express personal point of view		•	•	•	•	•
• Identify the point of view of the author or a character		•	•	•	•	•
• Distinguish between fact and fiction using evidence from the story, article		•	•	•	•	

Literature Response Forms

Table of Contents

Teacher Assessment Rubric

Name: _____

Date: _____

Put a check mark in the box that indicates the student's level of achievement.

Level 1 - requires assistance, inconsistent effort, shows limited understanding of concepts
Level 2 - requires minimal assistance, shows limited understanding of concepts
Level 3 - independent, consistent effort, shows general understanding of concepts
Level 4 - independent, consistent effort, shows thorough understanding of concepts

Criteria	Level 1	Level 2	Level 3	Level 4
Vocabulary Development				
• Understands the text at word level.				
• Recognizes and understands figurative and expressive language.				
Identifying Important Information				
• Identifies the message, main idea, and supporting details.				
• Evaluates story elements and conclusion.				
• Draws conclusions based on personal interpretation.				
Character Analysis				
• Demonstrates an understanding of character traits.				
• Uses knowledge of character roles to evaluate roles and gives supporting details.				
Summarizing Events				
• Retells a story in proper sequence with supporting details.				
• Identifies and describes story elements.				
Reasoning and Critical Thinking				
• Makes connections between text and the real world.				
• Makes judgements and draws conclusions using evidence from the story.				
• Uses evidence to make predictions and inferences.				
• Develops opinions and expresses personal point of view.				
Creativity and Design				
• Create a text form: theatrical script, story wheel.				
• Creates a media text form: advertisement, poster.				
• Express own interpretation through visual and performing arts.				

Comments:_____

_____

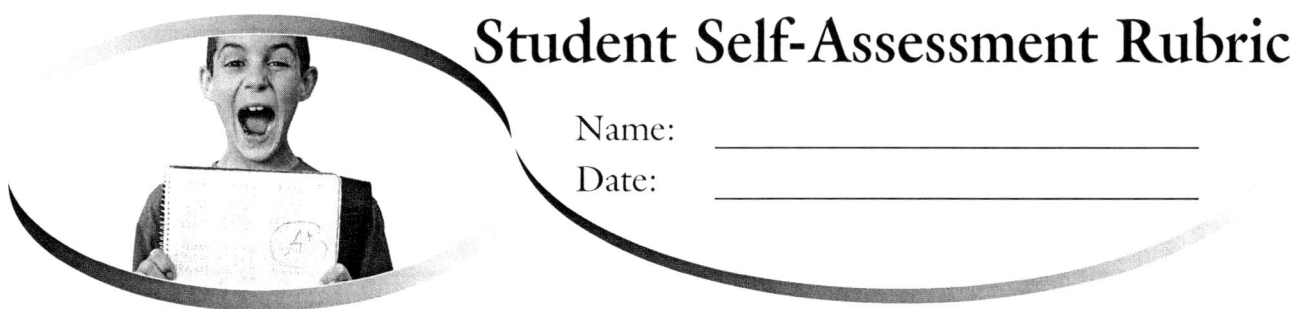

Student Self-Assessment Rubric

Name: _____

Date: _____

Put a check mark in the box that best describes your performance, then add your points to determine your total score.

Expectations	Actual Performance (measured in points)				
	1 Needs Improvement	2 Sometimes	3 Frequently	4 Always/almost always	Points
✔ I remained focused and on task.					
✔ I asked for explanations and assistance when needed.					
✔ I was prepared and organized.					
✔ I used my text to support ideas.					
✔ I used my own experiences and knowledge to support my predictions.					
✔ I used all available resources.					
✔ I chose a variety of texts for my activities.					
✔ I rechecked the information so I could rethink my answers.					
✔ I edited and proofread my work.					
✔ I know what I am good at.					
✔ I know what I need to work on.					

Total Points: _____

The most valuable thing I learned was _____

_____

_____

Literature Response Forms

Introduction:

Students acquire their essential knowledge and skills about reading during their primary and junior years. These skills include the ability to comprehend, analyze, evaluate, and create. They experience a number of ways to reflect upon what they have read. Students in Grades 6, 7, and 8 require opportunities to build upon this foundation to consolidate and extend their language skills.

Planning and Implementation Guide

1. **Why Use Literature Response Forms?**

    *   Responding to literature is a process in which the learner derives meaning from a variety of texts. It involves thinking about that text before, during and after the actual follow-up activity. Because reading comprehension is a thought process, assessment can be done indirectly.

    *   Literature response forms help the teacher to assess student understanding of the different forms of texts that they are encountering. The activities in this resource encourage students to make creative connections between their previous learning and the text form. These connections strengthen and extend their level of reflection.

    *   Literature response forms offer meaningful, appealing activities that students can complete independently during English class. This provides classroom time for you to conduct small group instruction, assist other students or to conference with individual students.

    *   These worksheets provide accurate assessment information on student skill levels. An analysis of completed activities will assist you in determining the next steps in your planning and programming to meet individual student needs.

2. **Introducing Literature Response Forms in a Mini-Lesson**

    *   Literature response forms should be introduced to the whole class after a discussion of a variety of text forms within their scope of reading. For the initial mini-lesson, select a literature form that supports the skill focus of the worksheet you are introducing.

    *   Step by step teach your students the skill focus of the response form by using an enlarged copy of the worksheet: overhead, chart paper or chalkboard. Explain the concepts being introduced, using the "think aloud" strategy to model your thinking as you complete the form. Students can see and understand the process you go through to respond. Involve the students in a guided practice by asking them questions, encouraging discussion, and recording a variety of their responses. Be sure to highlight the range of possibilities of appropriate responses.

Literature Response Forms

- After the mini-lesson, have the students practice completing the worksheet as a response to a chosen text form.

- Use this mini-lesson format to introduce each new literature response form.

- Teach and model several response forms, giving the students sufficient practice to work through them. Now you have created an independent literature activity. The students' results for shared, guided or independent comprehension can be used for your assessment records.

- Individual and collective learning needs of your students should direct the introduction of the response forms. Introducing worksheets from all six skill areas will assist students to develop a range of skills at varying levels of difficulty.

3. **Organizing Literature Response Forms**

   Literature response forms can be organized in a variety of different ways.

   - Students can be given a package/folder of literature response forms to complete within a specified time frame during English class. You may wish to designate the number of worksheets that must be completed.

   - The worksheets may be kept in labelled folders or bins, and students may be given a free choice to select the response form that best suits their chosen text form. Encourage students to vary their selections of print form. Ensure that students are aware of how many forms they must complete and how much time they have to complete the tasks.

   - The response forms can also be used to show a similar response to different text forms.

   - Intermediate students need to see their tasks as meaningful. In order to motivate them, alternate the response forms that are available so that they can practice, master and extend a variety of skills.

4. **Sharing Responses**

   - Allow time for students to share their responses so that they may celebrate their accomplishments. Sharing helps to develop motivated learners who acquire new ideas from peers and recommend reading materials to each other. Sharing also helps to foster self-confidence in individual students as they present and discuss their responses.

   - Sharing can be done weekly, as a whole class, or through individual assignments. Presentations can be made to the whole class or to small groups. Displaying student work on bulletin boards increases the sharing of ideas.

Literature Response Forms

5. **Helping Students Select Appropriate Reading Texts**

   - **Shared Reading** or **Reading Aloud:** These texts can be at any reading level as the teacher is reading the text and modeling the process to the students.

   - **Guided Reading:** Provide texts that are slightly harder than text that can be read independently. Students will receive teacher guidance and support during the lesson.
   This will enable some students to "stretch" their thinking with minimal risk.

   - **Independent Reading** or **Novel Study:** Help students to pick material that is at the "just right" level. For most students, this means reading on their own, with 95% accuracy. If the student makes more than five reading errors on the first page, then the text is too difficult.

6. **Examples of Materials to be Read:**

   Intermediate students have the skills and desire to expand their reading repertoire. It is important that they have access to a wide range of texts that are interesting and that are relevant to their personal experiences. Additionally, these texts should vary in length, form, and theme.

   Some suggestions are:
   - historical fiction, science fiction, realistic fiction, adventure, mystery
   - memoirs, autobiographies, biographies
   - satire, essays, reviews, editorials, letters to the editor
   - speeches, debates, presentations
   - song lyrics, plays, radio programs, and ads
   - magazines, newspapers, internet articles
   - maps, graphs,
   - non-fiction materials, cookbooks

7. **Tracking, Assessment, and Individual Programming**

   - The **Personal Reading Record** (p.11) and **Literature Response Tracking Sheet** (p.12) are to be completed by each student independently. These are useful tools for monitoring independent response activity and skill area completion.

   - A collection of the student's completed literature response forms provides an extensive overview of his/her reading comprehension skills. **Student-Teacher Conferences** may be conducted to gather information, performance-based assessment information, and direct individual programming. (form p. 9)

   - The **assessment rubrics** (p.4 and 5) are useful aides for gathering information on a student's strengths and needs. These rubrics should be used to direct independent instruction and mini-lessons. They will also provide feedback to students on their progress and guide them in setting personal learning goals.

Teacher - Student Conference Form

Student's Name: _____ **Date:** _____

Title: _____ **Chapter/Section:** _____

Record of Student's Retelling:

- Identifies setting, time, and place.   Yes ☐ No ☐
- Names primary and secondary characters.   Yes ☐ No ☐
- States main character's problem.   Yes ☐ No ☐
- Explains character's actions.   Yes ☐ No ☐

- Identifies main idea and provides supporting details.   Yes ☐ No ☐
  Comments: _____
  _____

- Describes the plot details in sequential order.   Yes ☐ No ☐
  Comments: _____
  _____

- Makes inferences.   Yes ☐ No ☐
  Comments: _____
  _____

- Makes connections with the text.   Yes ☐ No ☐
  Comments: _____
  _____

Additional Comments: _____
_____
_____
_____

Literature Response Forms

List of Work Sheets

Vocabulary Development
1. Check Out the Basics
2. Know What I Mean?
3. In Other Words
4. It's How You Say It
5. Excuse Me!
6. The Same as ….
7. Almost Human
8. Picture This
9. I Stand for ….
10. Idioms! Idioms! Everywhere!
11. Shish! Boom! Bah!
12. Remember Me?

Character Analysis
1. Good Guy, Bad Guy
2. That Character and You
3. You Read It Here
4. Character Web
5. Feelings from the Heart
6. Got Problems?
7. They Did What?
8. What a Character!
9. There's a Change in You
10. Dynamite Diamante!

Reasoning and Critical Thinking
1. Fact? Opinion?
2. How Do You Feel?
3. What If?
4. What's the Reason?
5. Please Tell Me
6. In Review
7. Theme
8. True Meaning
9. It Ends Like This
10. Conflict Resolved

Identifying Important Information
1. What's It All About?
2. Coming Up Next
3. Just Because
4. It Goes Like This
5. Top Four
6. Conflict
7. What Do You Really Mean?
8. Listen to the Clues
9. Get in the Mood
10. Let Me Think

Summarizing Events
1. In the First Place
2. Step into My Web
3. Before and After
4. It's About Time
5. Follow Me
6. Rhyme Time
7. In My Opinion
8. Perspectives in Contrast
9. The Way I See It
10. The Play's the Thing

Creativity and Design
1. Coming Soon!
2. Breaking News
3. Same Story, Different Place
4. Read This
5. I'm Puzzled!
6. Mapping the Way
7. Character ID
8. Say What?
9. Watch Closely
10. Where the Action Is

Personal Reading Record

_____'s Reading Record   Date _____

Date	Title	Author	Genre	#Pages

Genre Key: **F - Fiction**   **NF - Nonfiction**   **P - Poetry**   **O - Other (explain)**

Literature Response Tracking Sheet

Name: _____

Color the box of each completed activity.

Vocabulary Development
- ☐ 1. Check Out the Basics
- ☐ 2. Know What I Mean?
- ☐ 3. In Other Words
- ☐ 4. It's How You Say It
- ☐ 5. Excuse Me!
- ☐ 6. The Same as ….
- ☐ 7. Almost Human
- ☐ 8. Picture This
- ☐ 9. I Stand for ….
- ☐ 10. Idioms! Idioms! Everywhere!
- ☐ 11. Shish! Boom! Bah!
- ☐ 12. Remember Me?

Character Analysis
- ☐ 1. Good Guy, Bad Guy
- ☐ 2. That Character and You
- ☐ 3. You Read It Here
- ☐ 4. Character Web
- ☐ 5. Feelings from the Heart
- ☐ 6. Got Problems?
- ☐ 7. They Did What?
- ☐ 8. What a Character!
- ☐ 9. There's a Change in You
- ☐ 10. Dynamite Diamante!

Reasoning and Critical Thinking
- ☐ 1. Fact? Opinion?
- ☐ 2. How Do You Feel?
- ☐ 3. What If?
- ☐ 4. What's the Reason?
- ☐ 5. Please Tell Me
- ☐ 6. In Review
- ☐ 7. Theme
- ☐ 8. True Meaning
- ☐ 9. It Ends Like This
- ☐ 10. Conflict Resolved

Identifying Important Information
- ☐ 1. What's It All About?
- ☐ 2. Coming Up Next
- ☐ 3. Just Because
- ☐ 4. It Goes Like This
- ☐ 5. Top Four
- ☐ 6. Conflict
- ☐ 7. What Do You Really Mean?
- ☐ 8. Listen to the Clues
- ☐ 9. Get in the Mood
- ☐ 10. Let Me Think

Summarizing Events
- ☐ 1. In the First Place
- ☐ 2. Step into My Web
- ☐ 3. Before and After
- ☐ 4. It's About Time
- ☐ 5. Follow Me
- ☐ 6. Rhyme Time
- ☐ 7. In My Opinion
- ☐ 8. Perspectives in Contrast
- ☐ 9. The Way I See It
- ☐ 10. The Play's the Thing

Creativity and Design
- ☐ 1. Coming Soon!
- ☐ 2. Breaking News
- ☐ 3. Same Story, Different Place
- ☐ 4. Read This
- ☐ 5. I'm Puzzled!
- ☐ 6. Mapping the Way
- ☐ 7. Character ID
- ☐ 8. Say What?
- ☐ 9. Watch Closely
- ☐ 10. Where the Action Is

Teacher Notes:

Importance of Vocabulary Development

Primary and Junior students acquire word skills and strategies to derive meaning from words. While the expectation is for Intermediate students to build upon these skills, it should be remembered that the level of achievement of the students varies greatly.

This section will include:
- A review of prior skills and knowledge
- An introduction to figurative language.

Students may require a formal lesson for some skills before attempting the response activity.

Activities and Skills Covered in This Section:

Activity#	Name of Activity	Skill Focus
1.	Check Out the Basics	Nouns, Adjectives, Verbs, Adverbs
2.	Know What I Mean?	Prior Knowledge, Dictionary, Thesaurus
3.	In Other Words	Paraphrasing
4.	It's How You Say It	Types of Sentences and Their Purpose
5.	Excuse Me!	Interjections
6.	The Same as ….	Similes, Metaphors
7.	Almost Human	Personification
8.	Picture This!	Imagery
9.	I Stand for ….	Symbolism
10.	Idioms! Idioms! Everywhere!	Idioms
11.	Shish! Boom! Bah!	Onomatopoeia
12.	Remember Me?	Review of terms: word puzzle

Modeling a Literature Response Activity

Mini Lesson for: In Other Words (Page 16)

- Discuss some oral examples of rewording.
- Discuss the meaning of the term "paraphrase" and the conditions of accurate paraphrasing (see notes on worksheet)
- Give students a practice sheet with a paragraph to paraphrase. Stop halfway through the exercise to do "Think, Pair Share." Focus on meeting the conditions on accurate paraphrasing.
- Give students a copy of **"In Other Words."**
- Stress the importance of reading the given information and doing the lead-in exercise before attempting the activity as it relates to their individual stories.

Name: _____

Date: _____

Title: _____

Author: _____

Check Out the Basics

Every good author uses interesting basic vocabulary: **nouns, adjectives, verbs, and adverbs.**

Choose a section of your story to find proof of good basic words.
Write your answers on the chart below.
Find **6** examples for each part of speech.
Record the page number where you found each example.

Nouns: name a person, place or thing	**Page #**	**Adjectives:** describe nouns	**Page #**
1.		1.	
2.		2.	
3.		3.	
4.		4.	
5.		5.	
6.		6.	
Verbs: action words, "doing"	**Page #**	**Adverbs:** describe the action	**Page #**
1.		1.	
2.		2.	
3.		3.	
4.		4.	
5.		5.	
6.		6.	

inflection
flotation
diabolic
churl

Name: _____

Date: _____

Title: _____

Author: _____

Know What I Mean?

When we read a story, we sometimes find words whose **meanings** are strange to us.

Choose a section of your story for this activity.
Find **6** words whose **meanings** are unfamiliar to you. **Write** them on the chart.
Using your word skills, **write your idea** of the **meaning**.
Check a dictionary and then **write that meaning** for each word.

	Word	What I think it means	Dictionary meaning
1.			
2.			
3.			
4.			
5.			
6.			

A **thesaurus** is a dictionary that gives us **synonyms** and **antonyms**.

Choose 6 words from your story to **write** on the chart.
Write a **synonym** and **antonym** for each word.
Use a **thesaurus** if you need help.

	Word	Synonym	Antonym
1.			
2.			
3.			
4.			
5.			
6.			

Name: _____

Date: _____

Title: _____

Author: _____

In Other Words

As readers, we may not be clear as to exactly what the author is saying. Sometimes we may have to think about a passage in our own words in order to understand what has been said.

To **paraphrase** is to **restate** the thought of a passage in more **simple** and **clear language**. **Paraphrasing** makes the message more understandable.

A good paraphrase must:
- be clear and easy to understand
- contain all the ideas of the original passage
- not contain any ideas that were not in the original

Choose a short paragraph from your story that you found unclear. Copy the paragraph onto the lines below.

_____

_____

_____

_____

_____

_____

_____

_____

_____

Rewrite the paragraph in your own words so that the message is clearer.

_____

_____

_____

_____

_____

_____

_____

_____

_____

Name: _____

Date: _____

Title: _____

Author: _____

It's How You Say It

A good author will use a variety of sentence types when writing a story. Each type of sentence has a different purpose and punctuation.

An **assertive** sentence states a fact. **"The heart is a mighty pump."**

An **imperative** sentence gives a command. **"Check to make sure the campfire is out."**

An **interrogative** sentence asks a question. **"Have you ever gone camping?"**

An **exclamatory** sentence expresses strong emotion. **"What an amazing baseball game!"**

Choose a section of your story to look for different kinds of sentences. Find **3** examples of each type of sentence. **Record** your answers on the chart.

Assertive Sentences	Page #
1.	
2.	
3.	
Imperative Sentences	
1.	
2.	
3.	
Interrogative Sentences	
1.	
2.	
3.	
Exclamatory Sentences	
1.	
2.	
3.	

blow a fuse

break the news

eat your heart out

bring down the house

Name: _____

Date: _____

Title: _____

Author: _____

Excuse Me!

Wow! GREAT! Oh, no! Surprise!

Interjections are words that express strong feelings or sudden emotion.

They are usually followed by an **exclamation mark**.

"Super! Our team won!"

Sometimes they are followed by a **comma** and are part of the sentence.

"Oh, stop complaining."

Interjections are most effective when they are not over-used.

Choose a section of your story to look for different examples of interjections.
Find **6** examples of interjections in the text.
Record your answers on the chart.
Copy the interjection and the sentence that follows it.

Examples of Interjections	Page #
1.	
2.	
3.	
4.	
5.	
6.	

In your opinion, does this author use interjections wisely? Give a reason for your answer.

_____

_____

Name: _____

Date: _____

Title: _____

Author: _____

The Same as ....

When authors want to make comparisons, they often use **similes** or **metaphors**.

A **simile** is a comparison between two things that do not seem to be connected. Similes begin with *like*, as or *seems*.

"As I daydreamed, my mind floated like a fluffy white cloud."

A **metaphor** is a comparison that uses no connecting words. Readers have to make the comparison on their own.

"Memories are mirrors in our minds."

Often we have to put our own meaning on similes and metaphors. Decide if these expressions are a simile or a metaphor. **Rewrite** these similes and metaphors in your own words.

1. He had a deer-in-the-headlights look.   simile   metaphor

_____

2. Mom was as relaxed as a poached egg on toast.   simile   metaphor

_____

Look in your story for some examples of similes and metaphors.
Write your examples on the chart. Tell if the example is a simile or metaphor.
Write your meaning for the expression.

Expression from Story	Simile or Metaphor	My Meaning for this Expression

What has ears
but cannot hear?

Name: _____

Date: _____

Title: _____

Author: _____

Almost Human

There are many examples of **personification** in literature. Fables, fairy tales, and many animal stories use this form of language.

Personification gives **human qualities** or **actions** to something that is not human. Animals, inanimate objects, and even ideas can all be personified.

Many riddles are based on personification combined with word play.

Try to answer these:

1. What has eyes but cannot see? _____

2. How can you tell the difference between two types of trees? _____

3. What did one potato chip say to the other? _____

Look in your story for examples of **personification**: animals or objects have been given human thoughts, feelings, attitudes or actions.

Example of personification	I know that this is an example of personification because .....

Answers to riddles:
1. a potato
2. You listen to their bark
3. "Time for a dip!"

Name: _____

Date: _____

Title: _____

Author: _____

Picture This!

Settings, character descriptions, and stories about nature have many examples of imagery.

Imagery refers to words or phrases that help us to imagine what someone or something is like.

Imagery helps readers to form a **mental picture** of sights, sounds, smells, tastes, and feelings.

Skim over your story to find one or two paragraphs that you think are very descriptive.

Copy the paragraph(s) onto the lines below.

_____
_____
_____
_____
_____
_____
_____
_____
_____
_____
_____
_____
_____
_____

Use a highlighter to mark the descriptive parts of the paragraph.

Write examples of imagery from your highlighted notes. Tell what sense or feeling they appeal to.

_____
_____
_____
_____
_____
_____
_____

Name: _____

Date: _____

Title: _____

Author: _____

I Stand for ....

Many stories use **symbolism** to strengthen their message and make their ideas more appealing.

Symbolism is language that uses something concrete to stand for something vague or abstract. A **symbol** may be a **person, place** or **thing**. The symbol may stand for **an attitude, an idea, a feeling** or **a belief**. The symbol stands for something else, but it still keeps its own meaning.

Many symbols are so well known in our culture that we recognize the message right away. Match these symbols with their meanings. Choose a meaning from the box and write it beside its symbol.

national pride	poison	good luck	peace	old age	love

1. a dove _____ **2.** horseshoe _____

3. a heart (shape) _____ **4.** winter of one's life _____

5. skull and crossbones _____ **6.** our flag _____

Look in your story for some examples of symbolism.

Record your examples. Then explain the meaning of the symbolism in your example.

Example of Symbolism	Meaning of the Symbolism

Name: _____

Date: _____

Title: _____

Author: _____

Idioms! Idioms! Everywhere!

Oh! I have a splitting headache!   *It's right on the tip of my tongue.*

Chances are you know exactly what these expressions mean, even though you cannot take them to mean *exactly* what the words say.

An **idiom** is an expression that means something different from what it says. Idioms may mean something entirely different, or have no meaning at all, to someone from another culture. People who are learning the English language have difficulty with our idioms.

Idioms are usually used to add humor to a story. They create a picture in our mind with words.

Write your explanation of these common idioms.

1. Annie always makes a mountain out of a molehill

_____

2. You drive me up the wall.

_____

3. I'm sitting on top of the world.

_____

Look in your story for some examples of idioms.

Write the idiom and your meaning for it on the chart below.

Idiom from My Story	My Meaning for this Idiom

SNAP! POP! CRACK! BANG! BONG!

Name: _____

Date: _____

Title: _____

Author: _____

Shish! Boom! Bah!

Have you ever watched an action-filled cartoon or old movie that flashed words like POW! SPLAT! or BAM! every time the hero made a big move? In literature, authors use sound words in much the same way.

Onomatopoeia provides sound effects to the reader because the very word suggests its meaning. Words such as *plop! buzz! sizzle!* create a sound and a picture in our mind.

Use onomatopoeia to describe the following sounds.

1. a tap dripping _____

2. a person screaming _____

3. a doorbell ringing _____

4. firecrackers exploding _____

5. a baby crying _____

Look in your story for examples of **onomatopoeia**.
Record your examples on the chart.
Explain what occurrence the sound is referring to or suggesting.

Example of Onomatopoeia	Occurrence the Sound is Referring to or Suggesting
Example: Creak! Creak!	A gate is swinging in the breeze

Name: _____
Date: _____
Title: _____
Author: _____

Remember Me?

This puzzle is a review of the terms you have learned about in Vocabulary Development.
Think back or refer to your worksheets.
Use a dictionary if you need additional help.

Use the words in the Word Box for your answers.
Match the word to its meaning.

Word Box				
idiom	imagery	interjection	metaphor	onomatopoeia
paraphrase	personification	simile	symbolism	

Meaning												
An expression that means something different from what it says												
A comparison that uses *like*, as or seems												
Words or phrases that help us to imagine sights, sounds, smells, and tastes												
A comparison that uses no connecting words												
A person, place, thing, or action that stands for an idea, belief or feeling												
To restate the thought or idea of a passage in more clear and simple language												
Exclamatory words that express strong feelings or sudden emotion												
Words whose sound suggest its meaning												
Giving **human qualities** or **actions** to something that is not human, such as animals, inanimate objects, and ideas												

Teacher Notes:

Importance of Identifying Important Information

Intermediate students usually have the basic skills to identify main characters, describe the setting and retell the plot. Now they can begin to extend those skills to more advanced applications. Once again, it should be remembered that the level of achievement of the students varies greatly.

This section will include:
- A review of prior skills: main idea, predictions, cause and effect
- An extension of plot lines, setting, and conflict
- An introduction to literary techniques

Students may require a formal lesson for some skills before attempting the response activity.

Activities and Skills Covered in This Section:

Activity#	Name of Activity	Skill Focus
1.	What's It All About?	Main Idea
2.	Coming Up Next	Predictions
3.	Just Because	Cause and Effect
4.	It Goes Like This	Plot Lines
5.	Top Four	Scenes, Settings
6.	Conflict	Conflict and Resolution
7.	What Do You *Really* Mean?	Irony
8.	Listen to the Clues	Foreshadowing
9.	Get in the Mood	Mood
10.	Let Me Think	Reflections

Modeling a Literature Response Activity

Mini Lesson for: Listen to the Clues (Page 34)

- Present some oral examples of predicting what will happen next.
- Discuss the meaning of the term "foreshadowing" (see notes on worksheet)
- Give students a practice sheet with a paragraph to find examples of foreshadowing. Stop halfway through the exercise to do "Think, Pair, Share." Focus on how the foreshadowing is a clue to an upcoming event.
- Give students a copy of **"Listen to the Clues."**
- Stress the importance of reading carefully and relating the clues to what is already known.

Name: _____

Date: _____

Title: _____

Author: _____

What's It All About?

Titles can give clues about important ideas in a story or book.
Write the title of your book, story or chapter.

Title: _____

What clues did you get from this title?

_____

Does this title give you any clues to help you decide what the main idea is? Explain.

_____

_____

What is the main idea in this piece of literature?

_____

_____

Support your answer by describing four key events or details.

1. _____

_____

2. _____

_____

3. _____

_____

4. _____

_____

Think of the main idea as you write a new title for this text.

A good title might be _____ because

_____

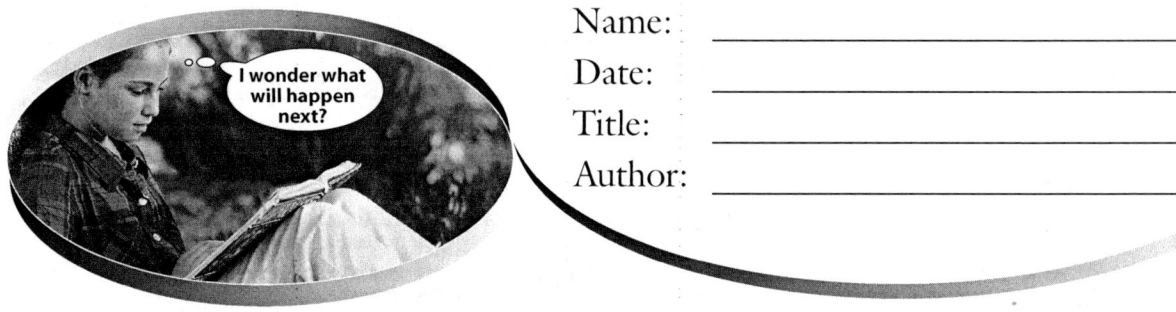

Name: _____

Date: _____

Title: _____

Author: _____

Coming Up Next

In many cases, an author will give the reader clues that lead us to make a **prediction** about what will happen next.

Select a section from your text that you think is a clue to an upcoming event in the story.

What has just happened?

_____

_____

What do you think will happen next?

_____

_____

What clues did the author give that would lead to this prediction?
Record the page numbers for the clues you found.

Clue	Page #
1.	
2.	
3.	

Did you use ideas from your own experience to make your prediction? Explain.

_____

_____

Continue reading until you find out if your prediction was correct. Were you correct? Explain.

_____

_____

_____

Name: _____

Date: _____

Title: _____

Author: _____

Just Because

A **cause** is the **reason** for an event occurring.

An **effect** is the **important event** that occurred.

Think about three important events that happened in your story. Select one from the **beginning, middle** and **end** of the text.

Describe these events in the **Effect** column.

Then write the reasons they happened in the **Cause** column. Consider the setting, the actions or thoughts of the characters, and any outside forces.

Effect: The event that occurred.	**Cause:** The reason this event occurred.
1. Beginning of the Story	**1.** Beginning of the Story
2. Middle of the Story	**2.** Middle of the Story
3. End of the Story	**3.** End of the Story

Name: _____

Date: _____

Title: _____

Author: _____

It Goes Like This

A **plot line** has five major parts: exposition, rising action, climax, falling action, resolution.

Rethink your text and **recall** the parts of the plot line.

Record examples from the text to match the category.

Elements of the Plot Line	Examples from your text to match this category
Exposition: the part of the story where characters are introduced. The setting is described and necessary information is given. • List major characters; describe the setting; relate background information	
Rising action: one or more conflicts are introduced into the story. This causes several difficulties to arise. • Give examples of some problems that arise. • Summarize one or more of the conflicts that occur.	
Climax: the point in the story where the action reaches its peak. Usually, it means that a turning point will follow soon. • Give a short summary of the high point in your story. • Tell what you think will be the turning point soon to follow.	
Falling action: the action or dialogue that comes after the climax. This part leads to the ending of the story. • Summarize the action and dialogue in your text that follows the climax.	
Resolution: the point at which all difficulties are resolved. The dialogue and action end. • Explain how the conflicts and problems were resolved.	

Name: _____

Date: _____

Title: _____

Author: _____

Top Four

Illustrate the following scenes using a variety of art medium: pencil, colored pencil, crayon, markers.

Complete the short **writing activity** for each scene.

Illustrate a scene showing the main character doing something that is important to the story line.	Illustrate the scene that you liked the best. Pick one that does not include a character.
In this scene, the main character is _____ _____ _____	This is one of my favorite scenes because _____ _____ _____
Illustrate a scene that you feel the author could have left out.	Illustrate a scene that reminds you of a place that you know of or you have visited.
I feel that this scene could have been left out of the story because _____ _____ _____	This scene reminds me of _____ _____ because _____ _____

Name: _____

Date: _____

Title: _____

Author: _____

Conflict

Conflict is created by a **problem** or **difficulty** within the story line.

Conflict can be **internal** or **external**.

External conflict can be:
- person vs. person
- person vs. nature
- person vs. society (against the accepted laws, rules or standards)
- fate (an unusual coincidence occurs)

Internal conflict is person vs. self. The character is torn in two (or more) different directions.

Conflict is essential to the plot and action of the story.

Think about the conflicts that have occurred in your story.

Record your answers on the chart.

What was the conflict about?	Who was involved in this conflict?

Name: _____

Date: _____

Title: _____

Author: _____

Oh! Great!

What Do You *Really* Mean?

Authors may use words or phrases when they want to say or mean something that is the **exact opposite** of the normal meaning.

For example: You spill chocolate milk on your shirt and then exclaim, "Oh! Great!!"

The types of irony are:

- **dramatic irony:** You, the reader, can see a character's mistakes and flaws but the character does not see them
- **verbal irony:** The writer says one thing and means another.
- **situational irony:** There is a noticeable difference between the character's reason for a particular action and the result of it.

Look in your text for some examples of **irony**.

Describe the situations and tell which type of irony it shows.

Situation from My Text	Type of Irony
1. _____ _____ _____	_____ _____
2. _____ _____ _____	_____ _____
3. _____ _____ _____	_____

Name: _____

Date: _____

Title: _____

Author: _____

Listen to the Clues

Foreshadowing is used to peak the reader's interest and entice us to keep on reading.

The author will give subtle clues or drop hints so we can predict facts about **characters** and their actions and about what may happen next in the **plot**.

Find hints in your story :
1. about the characters that lead you to predict something about their future actions.
2. about the events in the story that help you to predict what will happen next.

1. Hints About the Characters	My Predictions About How the Characters Will Act
Example: "In situations like this, Billy could be a hot-head."	Billy will probably get angry and start a fight.

2. Hints About the Plot	My Predictions About What Will Happen Next
Example: " I didn't think I was afraid until I heard that screeching sound behind me"	An animal or person may appear and danger is near.

Name: _____

Date: _____

Title: _____

Author: _____

Get in the Mood

Mood is the feeling you get when you are reading a story.

Examples: mysterious, excited, suspenseful, terrifying, thrilling, apprehensive

Mood can be created through the author's choice of **words** and **letter sounds**, and through **repetition of words, phrases and sentences**.

List situations from your text where the author is creating a certain mood by describing a character's actions or the events in the story.

Record the sounds, words, phrases, and sentences used to create the mood.

Tell the mood you think the author is creating.

Event or Character Being Described	Word Sounds	Words, Phrases, Sentences	Mood Being Created

Name: _____

Date: _____

Title: _____

Author: _____

Let Me Think

Most stories that we read leave an impression upon us. Often we relate details and events in the story to our own experiences and background.

Reflect upon your story by writing your thoughts in response to these questions.

1. What part of this story was most meaningful to you? Why?

   _____

   _____

   _____

   _____

2. What character or situation do you most identify with? Why?

   _____

   _____

   _____

   _____

3. Select a passage or quotation from the novel that you believe is important.

   Passage/quotation on page_____

   Briefly describe this passage or explain the quotation in your own words.
   Explain why you think it is important.

   _____

   _____

   _____

   _____

   _____

Teacher Notes:

Importance of Character Analysis

Intermediate students can readily identify main characters, describe what they look like and how they live. They will look at how characters solve problems and why they behave the way they do. Once again, it should be remembered that the level of achievement of the students varies greatly.

This section will include:

- A review of prior skills: main characters, character webs
- An extension of skills to character emotions, changes and problem solving.

Students may require a formal lesson for some skills before attempting the response activity.

Activities and Skills Covered in This Section:

Activity#	Name of Activity	Skill Focus
1.	Good Guy, Bad Guy	Protagonist/Antagonist
2.	That Character and You	Compare/Contrast
3.	You Read It Here	Analysis/Evaluation
4.	Character Web	Character Web
5.	Feelings from the Heart	Emotions
6.	Got Problems?	Problem Solving
7.	They Did What?	Character Actions
8.	What a Personality!	Character Sketch
9.	There's a Change in You	Character Changes
10.	Dynamite Diamante!	Character Diamante

Modeling a Literature Response Activity

Mini Lesson for: Dynamite Diamante! (Page 47)

- Discuss the meaning of the form of poetry named *diamante*
- Outline the structure for writing a diamante. Display the outline on a chart or chalkboard so students may refer to it.
- Give students a copy of the sheet that they will be using for this activity.
- Instruct them to write a diamante about themselves, using the outline.
- Display their final products for others to read.
- Give students a copy of **Dynamite Diamante!** to complete for their story.

Name: _____

Date: _____

Title: _____

Author: _____

Good Guy, Bad Guy

An important feature of a good story is its characters. There are usually one or two major characters and a number of minor characters.

A **protagonist** is a principal character who plays a major part in developing the story.
He or she will be a leader whom we regard as a **hero** or **heroine**.
The protagonist may champion some cause, rescue someone or bring a villain to justice.

An **antagonist** is the character who opposes the protagonist and causes problems.
While the antagonist is an important part of the story, we regard him/her as a **villain**.
The villain is often overcome by the protagonist's thinking and actions.

Think about your story. Then answer the questions.

1. Who is the **protagonist** in this story? Explain your choice.

   _____

   _____

   _____

2. Who is the **antagonist** in this story? Explain your choice.

   _____

   _____

   _____

3. Describe the problems that the villain caused for the hero.

   _____

   _____

   _____

   _____

   _____

   _____

Name: _____

Date: _____

Title: _____

Author: _____

That Character and You

Think about the characters in your story. Select a character that you **disliked**.

Compare yourself to this character by using the Venn diagram below.
Summarize traits about yourself and this character in the outside circles.
Record the traits that you share in the overlapping section of the circle.

Include: personality, physical traits, actions, beliefs

The character I have chosen is _____

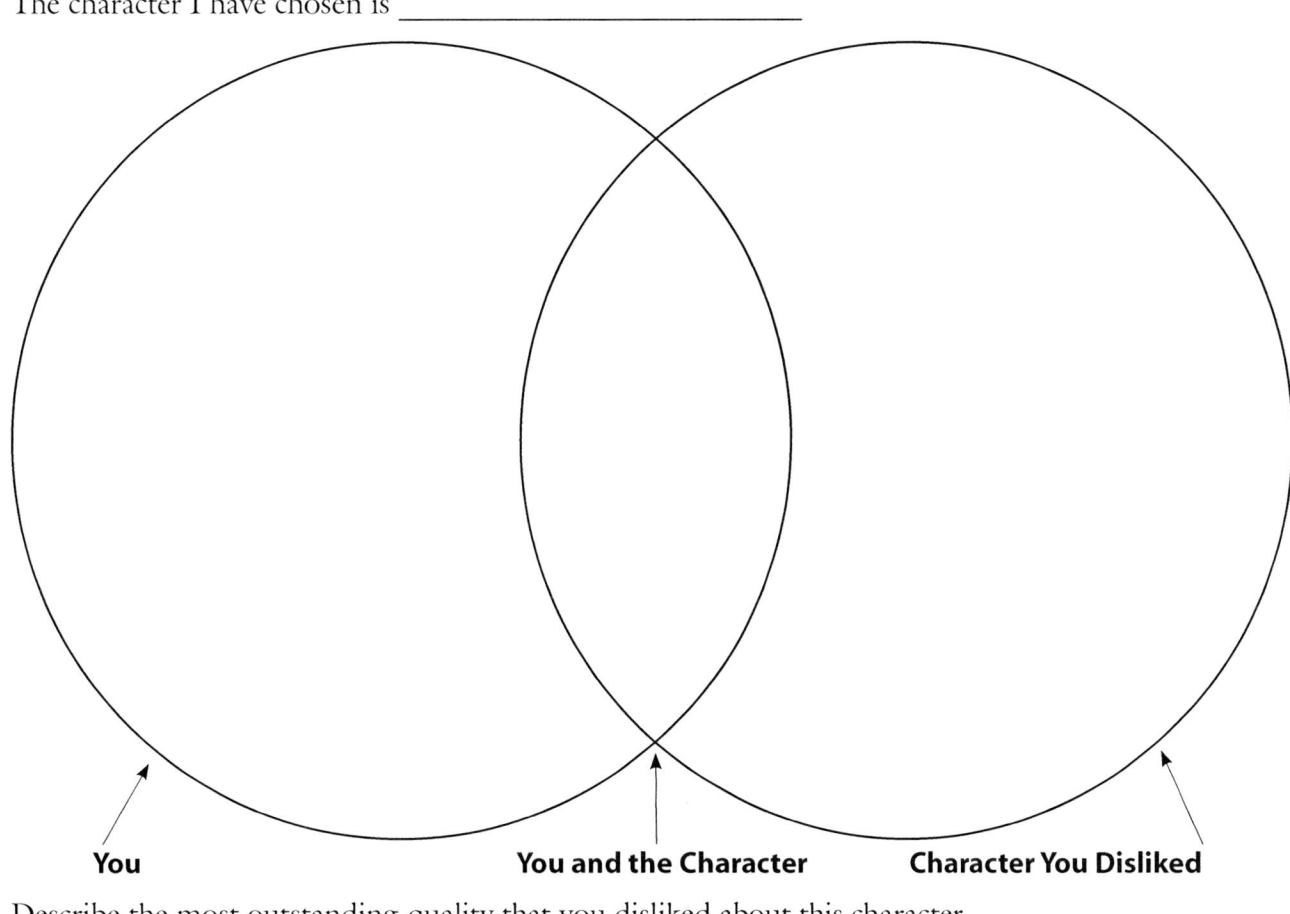

You   **You and the Character**   **Character You Disliked**

Describe the most outstanding quality that you disliked about this character.

_____

_____

_____

Name: _____

Date: _____

Title: _____

Author: _____

You Read It Here

Pretend you are a newspaper reporter who has been given an assignment covering the main character in your story.

The assignment requires you to include:
- a description of the character
- an outline of the problems faced by the character
- examples of the character's solutions to the problems
- your opinion of the character's ability to solve these problems
- whether or not you agree with the character's solutions. Give reasons.

Remember to consider the setting of the story when you write your report.

_____
_____
_____
_____
_____
_____
_____
_____
_____
_____
_____
_____
_____
_____
_____
_____
_____
_____
_____
_____
_____
_____

Name: _____
Date: _____
Title: _____
Author: _____

Character Web

Think about the characters in your story.

Select the main character and one other character for this activity.

- Use the webs below for your answers.
- Write the **name** of the character in the oval shape.
- On each line, write **one adjective** that describes the character.
- Under the adjective, write a **direct quote** from the story to support your choice.

Character 1: _____

Character 2: _____

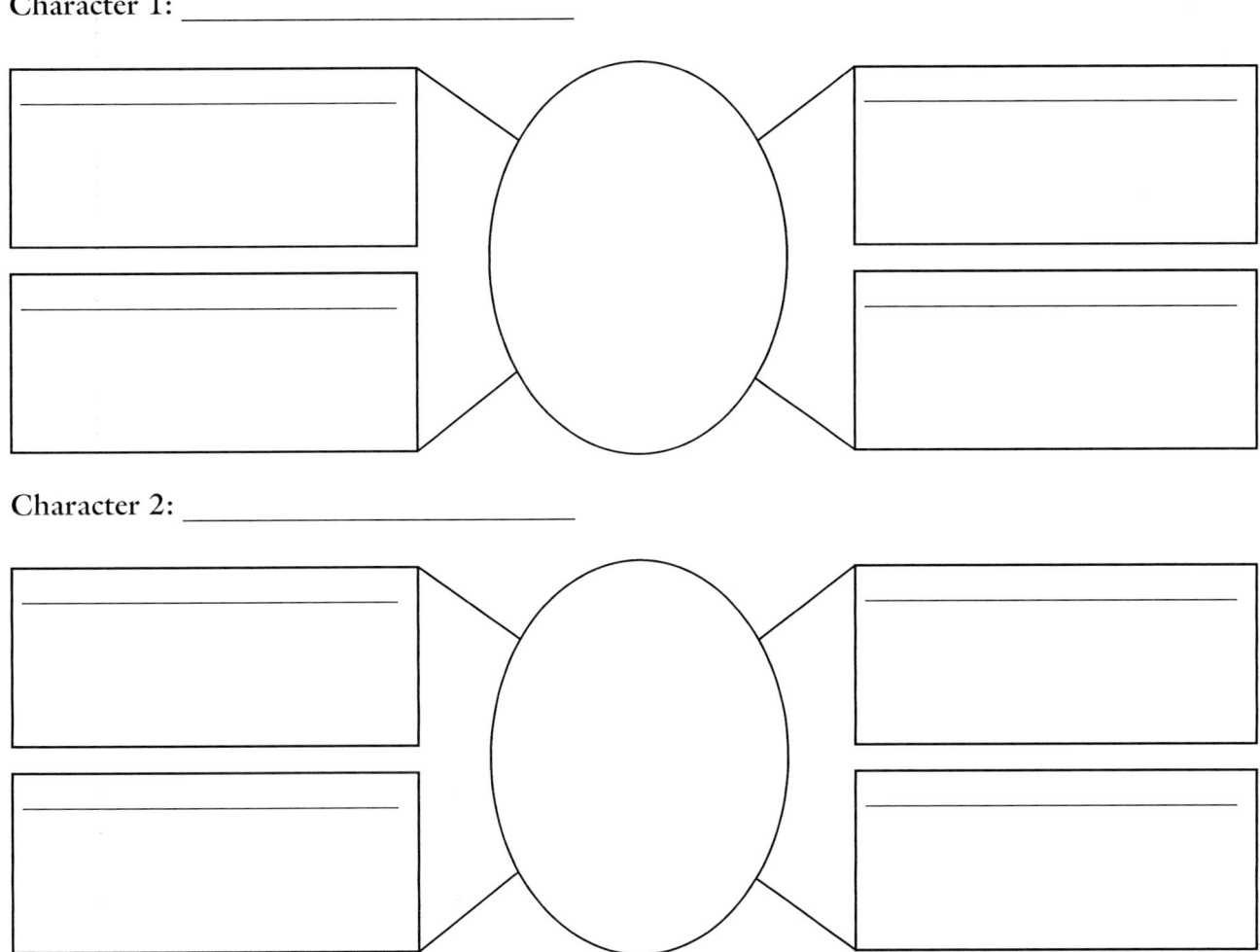

Name: _____

Date: _____

Title: _____

Author: _____

Feelings From The Heart

Characters will have different **emotions** as the story progresses.

Choose a selection from the **beginning**, the **middle** and the **end** of the story.

Summarize the events of each part.
Then summarize the character's emotions during each of these sections.

Beginning of the story _____

Description of the Scene	Summary of the Character's Emotions

Middle of the story _____

Description of the Scene	Summary of the Character's Emotions

End of the story _____

Description of the Scene	Summary of the Character's Emotions

Name: _____

Date: _____

Title: _____

Author: _____

Got Problems?

In most stories, the main character faces problems that have to be solved.

After the **climax** (the high point of interest), the problems are usually resolved.

1. What was the biggest problem that this character faced?

   _____

   _____

2. What methods did the main character use for solving the problem?

   _____

   _____

3. If you were faced with a similar problem, would you solve it in the same way? Tell why.

   _____

   _____

   _____

4. Compare your problem solving strategies with that of the main character.
   Give an example of a problem and tell how you would try to solve it.

Situation	Example	My Strategy for Solving It
When I have a problem with my friends		
When I have a problem at school		
When I have a problem with my family		

Name: _____

Date: _____

Title: _____

Author: _____

They Did What?

A character's actions and reactions often depend upon the type of personality they have.

A writer will portray different personalities to add interest to the story.

Think about the characters, and their personalities, in your story.

List the characters and your **opinion** of their personality.

Support your answer by **quoting a part** from the story.

Name of Character	Type of Personality (what they are like, how they behave)	Support For My Opinion Quote a part from the story

Name: _____

Date: _____

Title: _____

Author: _____

What a Character!

A **trait** is a word or phrase that describes a character's personality.

Pick a character from your story. Write the name: _____

Describe the physical appearance of this character by illustration and words.

My Illustration of My Character	My Written Description of His/Her Appearance
	_____ _____ _____ _____ _____ _____ _____

List three character traits for this person.

1. _____   2. _____   3. _____

Select **one trait** and **support** your choice with facts from the story.

Trait I Have Chosen	Character's Words	Character's Thoughts	Character's Actions
_____ _____	_____ _____ _____ _____	_____ _____ _____ _____	_____ _____ _____ _____

Name: _____

Date: _____

Title: _____

Author: _____

There's A Change In You

As a story progresses, a character may begin to undergo changes.

Think about the characters in your story.
How did they change as the story unfolded?

Record your answers on the chart.

Name of Character	Change in the Character's Words	Change in the Character's Thoughts	Change in the Character's Actions

In your opinion, which character changed the most? Give reasons for your answer.

_____

_____

_____

_____

_____

Name: _____
Date: _____
Title: _____
Author: _____

Dynamite Diamante!

Select the character from your story that held your interest the most.

Write a **character diamante poem**.

Follow the steps below for the correct structure.

    Line 1: the character's name

    Line 2: two adjectives to describe the character's personality

    Line 3: three –ing verbs that describe the character's actions

    Line 4: four nouns that name people, places, or things important to this character

    Line 5: one – ing verb and two adverbs that describe the character's actions

    Line 6: one adjective (ending in –ing) and one noun to describe a character feature

    Line 7: the character's name

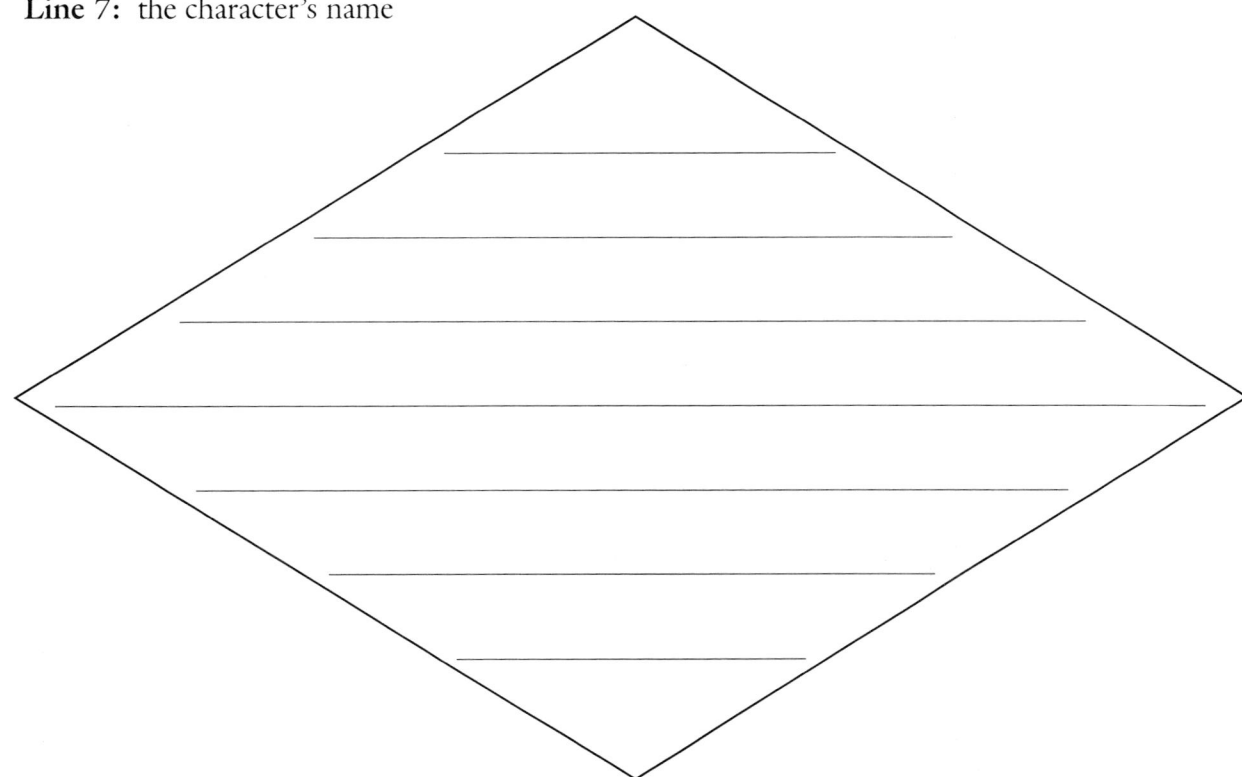

Teacher Notes:

Importance of Summarizing Events

Intermediate students should be able to summarize the main events and sequence their order. This provides a stepping stone to move onto other skills and aspects of story features, such as perspective and point of view. Once again, it should be remembered that the achievement level of the students varies greatly.

This section will include:
- A review of prior skills: sequence of events, setting, timelines
- An extension of skills to prologue/epilogue, perspective, point of view.

Students may require a formal lesson for some skills before attempting the response activity.

Activities and Skills Covered in This Section:

Activity#	Name of Activity	Skill Focus
1.	In the First Place	Sequence of Events
2.	Step Into My Web	Setting Web
3.	Before and After	Prologue/Epilogue
4.	It's About Time	Time Line
5.	Follow Me	Story Map
6.	Rhyme Time	Rhyming Couplets
7.	In My Opinion	Opinion - Essay
8.	Perspectives in Contrast	Perspective of Characters
9.	The Way I See It	Point of View
10.	The Play's The Thing	Scripting a Chapter

Modeling a Literature Response Activity

Mini Lesson for: Before and After (Page 5)

- Discuss the meaning of the terms prologue and epilogue.
- Give the students a short story to read and discuss.
- Instruct the class to write a prologue to the story. Stop part way through the exercise to do "Think, Pair Share."
- Repeat the exercise by having students write an epilogue. Do "Think, Pair, Share."
- Give students a copy of Before and After to complete for their story
- Stress the importance of succinct writing for this activity.

Name: _____

Date: _____

Title: _____

Author: _____

In The First Place

Characters will have different **emotions** as the story progresses.

Choose a selection from the **beginning**, the **middle** and the **end** of the story.

Summarize the events of each part.
Then summarize the character's emotions during each of these sections.

Beginning of My Story
Initially,
_____
_____
_____
_____
_____

Middle of My Story
Subsequently,
_____
_____
_____
_____
_____

End of My Story
In conclusion,
_____
_____
_____
_____
_____

Name: _____

Date: _____

Title: _____

Author: _____

Step Into My Web

We know that the **setting** refers to the **time** and **location** in which a story happens.
The setting details will influence the **thoughts** and **actions** of the **characters** and the **plot**.

Choose one section of the story that especially interested you.

Setting	
The time of this section is _____ _____ _____ _____ _____ _____	The place of this story is _____ _____ _____ _____ _____ _____
The time of this story is important to its plot development because _____ _____ _____ _____ _____ _____	The place of this story is important to its plot development because _____ _____ _____ _____ _____ _____

The **setting** details, **time** and **place** will have an influence on the main character.

Explain how the setting of this section causes the main character to think, act or behave as they do.

_____

_____

_____

_____

_____

Name: _____

Date: _____

Title: _____

Author: _____

Before and After

Some authors will write two short sections for their story: one will be at the beginning and one will be at the end. A story may have both sections or just one or the other, depending on the author's purpose for including them.

A **prologue** is a short **introduction** to the story.
- It comes just **before** the start of the story and is brief, usually one page in length.
- The speaker in the prologue can be the author or the main character.
- Its purpose can be to give a **personal comment** or **extra information** to the reader.

An **epilogue** is a short **conclusion** to the story.
- It comes just **after** the end of the story and is brief, usually one page in length.
- The speaker in the epilogue can be the author or the main character.
- Its purpose can be to **round out the story** or **summarize the main action**.

Write a prologue or an epilogue for your story.

Proloque/epilogue for ......

_____
_____
_____
_____
_____
_____
_____
_____
_____
_____
_____
_____
_____
_____
_____
_____
_____
_____
_____
_____

Owls in the Family
1. The boys found a baby owl
2. They built a cage for it
3. The owl became their pet

Name: _____

Date: _____

Title: _____

Author: _____

It's About Time

Each chapter of your story should contain at least one main event that contributes to the development of the story.

Make a **timeline** of your story by listing the main event for each chapter.
When you are finished, read over the list you have made.
Does it give an accurate summary of your story?

Chapter #	Main Event That Happens In This Chapter
1.	
2.	
3.	
4.	
5.	
6.	
7.	
8.	
9.	
10.	
11.	
12.	
13.	
14.	
15.	

If you require more room, use the back of your worksheet.

Name: _____

Date: _____

Title: _____

Author: _____

Follow Me

Create a story map by completing the outline below.

Main Characters: Choose three major characters from your story. Write a brief description for each one.		
Character #1	**Character #2**	**Character #3**

Setting #1: Describe the time and place where the story begins

Setting #2: Describe the time and place where the problem occurs

Problem: What was the problem? Who was involved?

How did the characters attempt to solve the problem?

Setting #3: Describe the time and place where the problem is solved

Solution: What was the best solution to this problem?

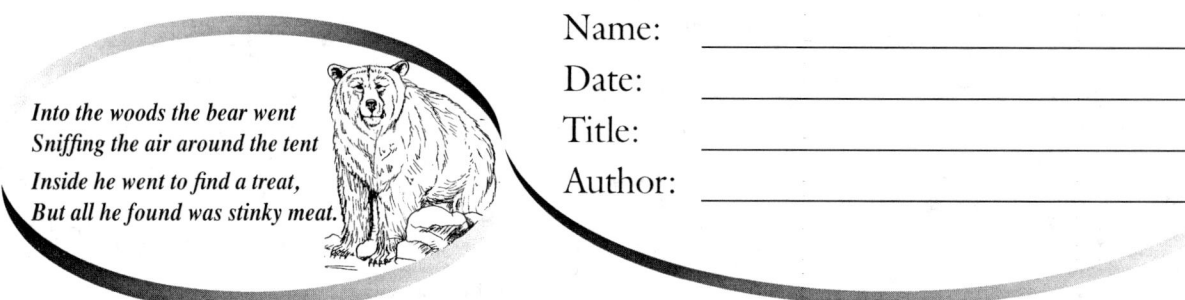

Into the woods the bear went
Sniffing the air around the tent

Inside he went to find a treat,
But all he found was stinky meat.

Name: _____

Date: _____

Title: _____

Author: _____

Rhyme Time

In Column 1, write **10 words** (nouns, verbs, adjectives, adverbs) that you consider important to the **plot** of your story.

In Column 2, write words that rhyme with the words in Column 1.

Choose at least five pairs of rhyming words from your list.
Write a **rhyming couplet** for each pair so that they retell your story.

Example: "We looked in through the open door,
And spied a map upon the floor."

	Column 1		Column 2
1.			
2.			
3.			
4.			
5.			
6.			
7.			
8.			
9.			
10.			

As you write your rhyming couplets, retell your story.

_____

_____

_____

_____

_____

Name: _____
Date: _____
Title: _____
Author: _____

In My Opinion

An essay is a short piece of writing that deals with one topic. It gives a personal view of a topic and can be in the form of a letter, speech, lecture or editorial.

The 5 paragraph essay follows this format:

Paragraph 1: **Introduction**
- Three or four general statements about the story.
- Thesis statement: this important sentence will give your argument for your opinion. Make this statement as forcible and clear as you can.

Paragraphs 2, 3, and 4: **Body**
- Topic sentence: sets the tone for the rest of the paragraph, lets the reader know what might be expected.
- Example to explain your topic sentence
- Support sentences (2) that give reason to your example
- Concluding sentence to sum up information for the reader

Paragraph 5: **Conclusion**
- Concluding sentences (2) to restate your ideas about the information in the Body.
- Final concluding sentence: restate the thesis to remind the reader of your opinion.

Pretend you are a speaker who has been asked to give your opinion about your book.

Decide on a **thesis statement**.

Example: "In my opinion, Sarah could have had a better relationship with her father."

My thesis statement: _____

_____

_____

Write a **5 paragraph essay** following the outline above.
Use examples from your story to support your argument.

Write your essay on a separate sheet of paper.

Name: _____

Date: _____

Title: _____

Author: _____

Perspectives in Contrast

Perspective in a story refers to
- mental images that bring awareness and comprehension.
- seeing ideas and relationships clearly
- assessing the relative importance and interrelation of events and character actions

Choose an **important event** that has an impact upon two characters in your story.
Write the names of the characters.

Write a **short summary** of the important event you have chosen.

Give you ideas about each **character's perspective** of the event: how the character views it.

Character 1		Character 2
Perspective	**Important Event**	**Perspective**

Did your characters have the same perspective on this event? Did they react the same or differently? Support your answer.

_____

_____

_____

_____

_____

Name: _____

Date: _____

Title: _____

Author: _____

The Way I See It

Point of view refers to how an author chooses to tell the story.

First person: one of the characters is telling the story.

Third person: a character from outside the story is telling the story.
- **Omniscient third person:** "all knowing." A narrator tells the story and tells what all characters think, do and feel. The narrator can read the minds of all characters.
- **Limited omniscient third person:** The narrator reads the mind of one character.

Think about your story.
What point of view was used to tell it? How do you know?
Give clues from your story that helped you decide.

_____

_____

_____

_____

Choose an important passage from your book.
Summarize what the author is saying.

Passage page _____

_____

_____

_____

_____

_____

Rewrite this summary using a different point of view.

_____

_____

_____

_____

_____

_____

Name: _____

Date: _____

Title: _____

Author: _____

The Play's The Thing

Select your favorite event or scene from the story; one that has 2 or 3 characters.

Rewrite the section in the form of a play or skit.

Include actions and gestures of your characters and any other information about the setting.

_____

_____

_____

_____

_____

_____

_____

_____

_____

_____

_____

_____

_____

_____

_____

_____

_____

_____

_____

_____

_____

_____

_____

_____

_____

_____

_____

_____

Teacher Notes:

Importance of Reasoning and Critical Thinking

Intermediate students need to become more skilled in their ability to analyze, synthesize and evaluate pieces of literature. This higher level of thinking and application will require guidance from the teacher and practice on the part of the students. As with other skills, it should be remembered that the achievement level of the students varies greatly.

This section will include:

- A review of prior skills: fact/opinion, emotions, alternate endings
- An extension of skills to theme, message, conflict resolution

Students may require a formal lesson for some skills before attempting the response activity.

Activities and Skills Covered in This Section:

Activity#	Name of Activity	Skill Focus
1.	Fact? Opinion?	Fact/Opinion
2.	How Do You Feel?	Emotions
3.	What If?	Alternate Ending
4.	What's the Reason?	Author Purpose
5.	Please Tell Me	Interview Questions
6.	In Review	A Review
7.	Theme	Theme
8.	True Meaning	Message/Meaning
9.	It Ends Like This	Evaluate an Ending
10.	Conflict Resolved	Conflict Resolution

Modeling a Literature Response Activity

Mini Lesson for: How Do You Feel? (Page 61)

- Brainstorm to create an extensive list of emotions. Record on a chart or chalkboard. Keep the list for future reference.
- Discuss the idea of emotions created by different parts of the same story.
- Give the class a short story to read. Choose a story that evokes different emotions.
- Assign single paragraphs to groups to discuss which emotion they felt and why.
- Record answers for everyone to see. Add a column for "How the author created this emotion."
- Co-operatively summarize and create a list of author techniques for creating emotions.

Fact? Opinion?

Many stories are a combination of factual information and someone's opinion.

Write eight statements that you feel tell important information about the characters, setting or plot.

Decide if the statements are fact or opinion. Explain your reasoning.

Statement	Fact	Opinion	My Reasoning
1.			
2.			
3.			
4.			
5.			
6.			
7.			
8.			

Name: _____

Date: _____

Title: _____

Author: _____

How Do You Feel?

While we are reading a story, we may experience a number of emotions.
A good author will try to create these feelings by the way they portray characters, how they describe a setting and how they develop the plot.

Choose three different examples from your text that caused you to feel some emotion.
Describe the character or setting or plot in each example.
Explain how the author created this emotion.

Description of Example	Emotion I Felt	How The Author Created This Emotion
1.		
2.		
3.		

Name: _____

Date: _____

Title: _____

Author: _____

What If?

Often while we are reading a story, we are able to predict how it will end. Sometimes we are surprised to find the story did not turn out as we had expected.

Summarize your story right up until the time where the problem appears.

Now continue writing to give your story a **different** and **original ending**.

Summary of the Plot	My New Ending
_____	_____
_____	_____
_____	_____
_____	_____
_____	_____
_____	_____
_____	_____
_____	_____
_____	_____
_____	_____
_____	_____
_____	_____
_____	_____
_____	_____
_____	_____
_____	_____
_____	_____
_____	_____
_____	_____

Name: _____

Date: _____

Title: _____

Author: _____

What's The Reason?

Authors have a variety of purposes in mind when they write a story.

- To entertain us
- To teach us something new
- To inform us
- To express an opinion
- To make us think about issues

Some stories will have more than one purpose.

Decide what **purpose** the author of your story was trying to achieve.

Write your opinion of this purpose, justifying it with examples from the text.

_____

_____

_____

_____

_____

_____

_____

_____

_____

_____

_____

_____

_____

_____

_____

_____

_____

_____

_____

Name: _____

Date: _____

Title: _____

Author: _____

Please Tell Me

Pretend you are interviewing someone who has also read your story.

Develop **seven interview questions** to determine the person's opinion of the book.

Ask **thought-provoking questions** about the characters, setting and plot.
Try to include ideas about the type of language used, the author's purpose and their opinion of the ending.

1. _____
   _____
   _____

2. _____
   _____
   _____

3. _____
   _____
   _____

4. _____
   _____
   _____

5. _____
   _____
   _____

6. _____
   _____
   _____

7. _____
   _____

Name: _____

Date: _____

Title: _____

Author: _____

In Review

As a member of the Library Club, it is your job to write reviews for the school newspaper.

Write a review of your book. Try to focus on
- Does the author develop believable characters?
- Is the plot original and does it hold your attention?
- Is the setting realistic and does it contribute to the story line?
- Are there intriguing details that make you want to continue to read?
- Would you recommend this book to other readers?

_____

_____

_____

_____

_____

_____

_____

_____

_____

_____

_____

_____

_____

_____

_____

_____

_____

_____

_____

_____

_____

Theme

Theme means an **idea** in literature that is a generalization about life, society, the world and even the universe.

Themes focus on **important ideas** and **ideals** and often are inspirational.

Example: People should be treated with respect regardless of race or religion.

Good authors create strong emotions through the theme in the minds of their readers.

State what you consider to be the theme of your story.

Support your ideas with examples and quotes from the text.

_____
_____
_____
_____
_____
_____
_____
_____
_____
_____
_____
_____
_____
_____
_____
_____
_____
_____
_____
_____

Name: _____
Date: _____
Title: _____
Author: _____

True Meaning

A good author will try to communicate a **message** to you through their story.

The **message** is the **underlying, deeper meaning** of the story.

Answer the questions to give your thoughts about the message in your story.

1. What do you consider to be the message in this story?

   _____

   _____

2. Does the title of the story give you any clues about the message? Explain.

   _____

   _____

3. What events contribute to the message?

   _____

   _____

   _____

   _____

4. What specific details contribute to the message?

   _____

   _____

   _____

   _____

5. In your opinion, does this author do a good job of getting the message across to you, the reader?
   Explain your thinking.

   _____

   _____

Name: _____

Date: _____

Title: _____

Author: _____

It Ends Like This

The conclusion or ending of a story should leave the reader with the feeling of completion.

The problems should be resolved, the plot is concluded and the characters are at peace.

Are you satisfied with the way your story ended? Did it conclude as you predicted it would?

Evaluate the ending of your story by
- describing the features you felt were well done and
- by outlining some suggestions you have for the author to make the ending more effective

a) Features that were well done:

_____

_____

_____

_____

_____

_____

_____

_____

_____

_____

b) Suggestions for a more effective ending

_____

_____

_____

_____

_____

_____

_____

_____

_____

_____

Name: _____

Date: _____

Title: _____

Author: _____

Conflict Resolved

A problem or **difficulty** that creates **conflict** exists within every story line.

Conflict can be **internal** or **external**.

External conflict can be: person vs. person, person vs. nature, person vs. society (against the accepted laws, rules or standards), fate (an unusual coincidence occurs).

Internal conflict is person vs. self. The character is torn in two (or more) different directions.

The way a conflict is solved is called the **resolution**. This is the part of the story where the major problem is solved and the story comes to a satisfactory end.

Conflict and **resolution** are essential to the plot and action of the story.

Think about the conflicts that have occurred in your story.

Record your answers on the chart. Use direct quotes from the story where possible.

What was the conflict about?	How was the conflict resolved?

Teacher Notes:

Importance of Creativity and Design

Intermediate students enjoy the opportunity to respond to literature in a variety of ways. By extending their thinking in the area of creative arts, they can produce results of a different type. The expectation is for Intermediate students to use their visual arts skills, and it should be remembered that the level of achievement of the students varies greatly.

This section will include:
- A review of prior skills and knowledge
- An introduction to realistic mapping, graphic novels

Students may require a formal lesson for some skills before attempting the response activity.

Activities and Skills Covered in This Section:

Activity#	Name of Activity	Skill Focus
1.	Coming Soon	Text to TV Show
2.	Breaking News!	Factual Report
3.	Same Story, Different Place	New Setting
4.	Read This	Theme
5.	I'm Puzzled	Visual/Written Summary
6.	Mapping the Way	Story Map
7.	Character ID	Character Description
8.	Say What?	Graphic Depiction with Dialogue
9.	Watch Closely	Text to TV Introductory Preview
10.	Where the Action Is	Visual Interpretation of the Climax of the Story

Modeling a Literature Response Activity

Mini Lesson for: Mapping the Way (Page 76)

- Explore some examples of maps and their uses.
- Discuss sources of maps: atlases, roadmaps, internet
- Give students a short story to read that involves a journey made by the main character.
- After discussing the story, co-operatively trace the route the character took.
- Give students a copy of **Mapping the Way** to complete for their own story.
- It may be beneficial for students to make notes about the character's journey as they read. This may make the mapping process easier for some students.

Name: _____

Date: _____

Title: _____

Author: _____

Coming Soon!

Pretend that you are working for a television network and your job is to create a television show based on a book. The first step is to develop the opening show for a mini series. You want to give people some information without giving away the whole story. Of course, you want to create interest in the audience as well.

Fill in the necessary information in the header.

Tell what you plan to include in the first show by writing a good description of the first section of the book.

Remember to create some interest at the end of the show to entice your audience to watch the next episode.

Name of This Episode: _____

Based on the Book: _____

Written by: _____

Starring: _____

_____

_____

_____

_____

_____

_____

_____

_____

_____

_____

_____

_____

_____

_____

_____

Name: _____

Date: _____

Title: _____

Author: _____

Breaking News!

Pretend you are a breaking news reporter for a local television station.

You have been sent to report on the latest developments in your story. The story is at its **high point** or **climax**.

Complete the outline below to provide the details of your on-the-spot report.

Good evening. This is .... **of** ....
    (your name)   (name of your tv station)

reporting live from the scene of ....
                                         (a scene from the setting of your story)

We have just learned that .... **has** ....
                                  (name of the character)   (describe the character's actions)

.... **Previously, it was thought that**

....
                          (outline the character's previous actions/thoughts)

We will be watching for .... **to** ....
                              (character's name)   (predict what you think the character will do next)

....

This is .... **with the latest news on this story. More updates**
            (your name)

will be coming to our audience as they become available.

Name: _____

Date: _____

Title: _____

Author: _____

Same Story, Different Place

Try to imagine the main character in your story in a different setting.

Create and illustrate a **new setting** for this plot. Include details that clearly show that this is a new and different place.

Then outline the changes your main character would have to make in order to adjust to this new environment.

New setting for _____

Changes the main character would have to make to adjust to this new setting:

_____

_____

_____

_____

_____

_____

_____

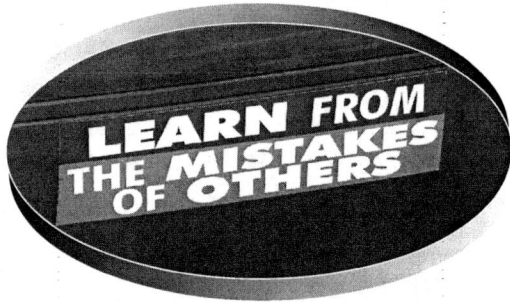

Name: _____

Date: _____

Title: _____

Author: _____

Read This

The **theme** of a story is the main idea turned into a generalization about life or the world.

Themes are important ideas written as short sentences or phrases. They are intended to inspire us towards better behavior and the common good.

Example: *"Do unto others as you would have them do unto you."*

Think about the main idea in the text you have just read. What is the main idea?

_____

_____

Write this idea as a short sentence or phrase.

_____

Design a bumper sticker that illustrates this theme.

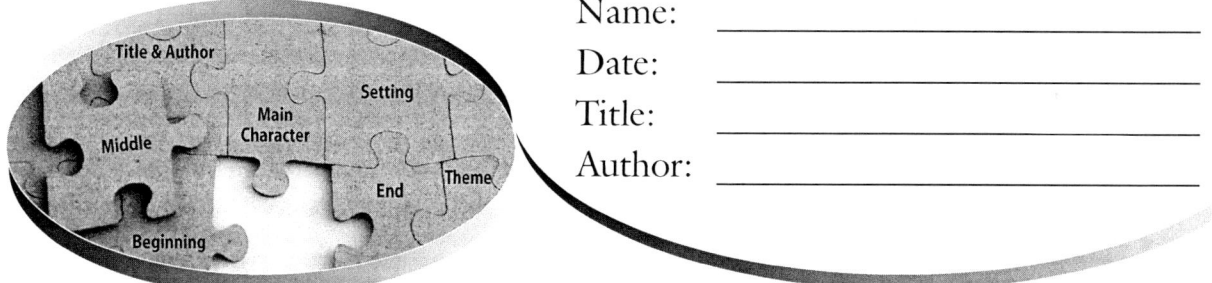

Name: _____

Date: _____

Title: _____

Author: _____

I'm Puzzled!

Create a puzzle for your story using the blank space below. Follow these steps.

- Divide the space into seven different parts. Use **straight lines**.
- Number the parts and outline each one with a dark color.
- Fill each space with **words** and **pictures** using this plan

Piece #1: the title and author of the book
Piece #2: short description of the main character (name, age, etc)
Piece #3: the setting (where, when)
Piece #4: beginning of the story (what happens)
Piece #5: middle of the story (what happens)
Piece #6: end of the story (what happens)
Piece #7: the theme of the story

- Cut out the pieces.
- Try retelling your story by putting the pieces back together.

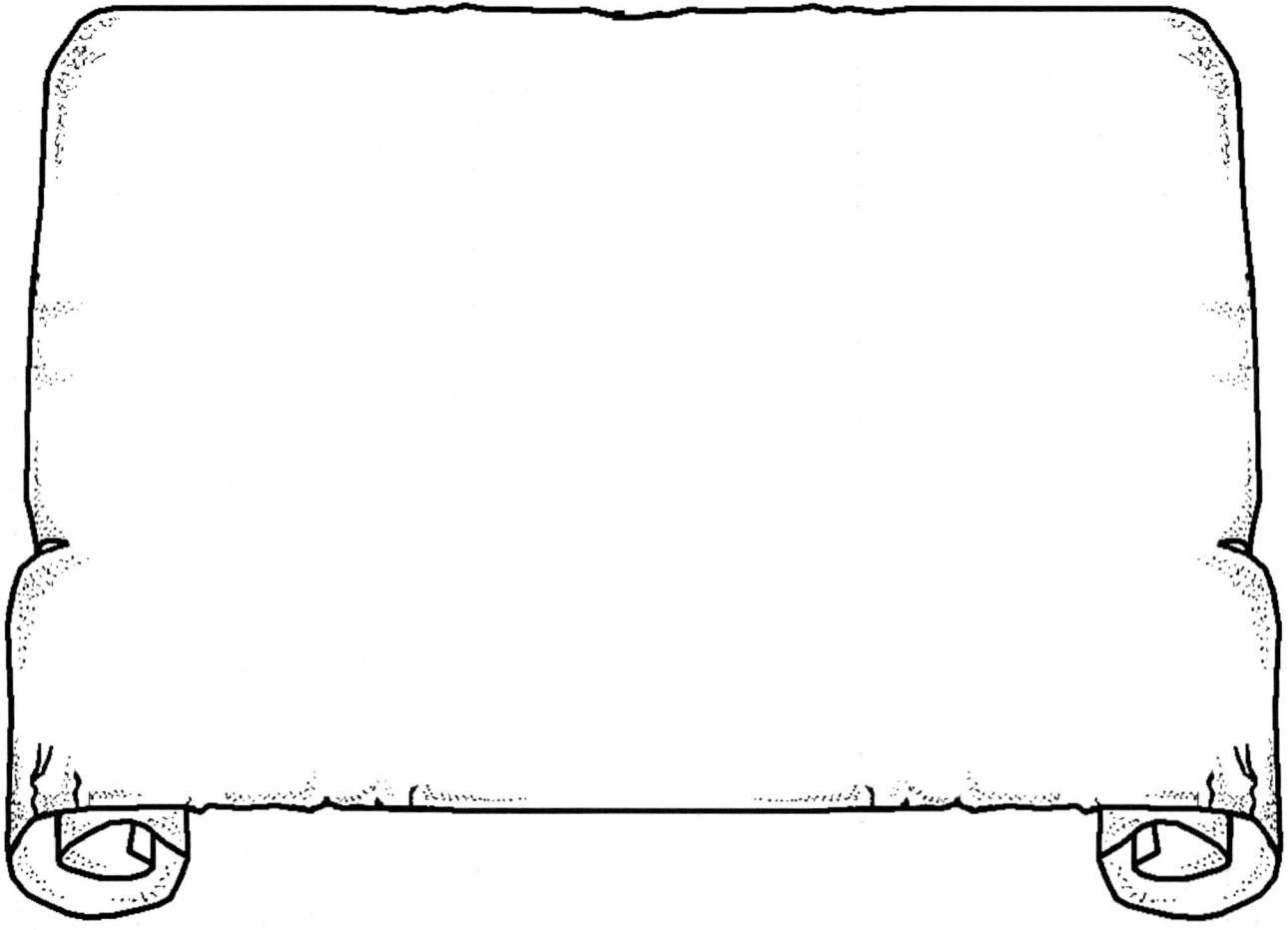

Name: _____

Date: _____

Title: _____

Author: _____

Mapping the Way!

You have seen maps in atlases, textbooks or looked at a roadmap while planning a trip.

A map can be helpful when reading a book to discover where the story is taking place.

Create a map to show the important places and the path the main character travels.

Use the space below or another, bigger sheet of paper.
- Decide where the main character starts out, where he or she goes, and where they end up.
- Find a map of that country, state or province. You could trace one from an atlas.
- **Trace** the character's route on your map.
- **Mark** the important places your character visited.
- **Number** the places in the order they appear in the story.

Name: _____

Date: _____

Title: _____

Author: _____

Character ID

Imagine that you work in a security division that makes ID cards for characters.

Create an ID card for your character using the form below.
- **Draw** and color a "shoulders and up" picture of the main character
- **Write** the character's name under the picture
- Complete the information on the other side of the card.
- Cut along the outside edges. Fold the card in half and glue the edges together.

Name: _____

Book Title: _____

Author: _____

Summary of what happens to this character in the story.

_____
_____
_____
_____
_____
_____
_____
_____
_____
_____
_____
_____

Name: _____

Date: _____

Title: _____

Author: _____

Say What?

A **graphic novel** tells a story by using pictures, speech balloons and some inserts with specific details. It resembles the comic book format.

Create a section of a graphic novel using this plan.
- Choose **one chapter** from your story. Use the chapter title or make up one of your own.
- Think about what happens in the beginning, middle and end of your chapter. This will help you to plan the frames.
- Illustrate the characters for each part. Use speech balloons for the characters' dialogue.
- To give some added written fact, draw a small box in the corner of the frame and write your information there.

Title: _____ Author: _____ Chapter Title: _____ _____	1.	2.
3.	4.	5.
6.	7.	8.

Name: _____
Date: _____
Title: _____
Author: _____

Watch Closely!

Pretend your book has recently been made into a movie.
You have the task of preparing an info ad for television to attract viewers.
Your ad needs to have a series of frames that will interest the viewer but not disclose the story.
Think about ads you have seen that make you want to watch a movie based on a book.

Make a draft of your ad by completing the frames below.

Frame #1: Use some opener like "Coming soon ...." with a picture that relates to the book

Frame #2: Title of the movie. It does not need to be the same as the book.
Follow with "Based on the book ...."

Frames #3 to 6: Illustrate the highlights of the story.

Under each illustration, write what the narrator will be saying as each picture appears on the television screen.

1.	2.	3.
4.	5.	6.

Name: _____

Date: _____

Title: _____

Author: _____

Where the Action Is

The climax is the **high point** in the story where the action is at its peak.
The story's events are most intense here and it signals that the story is **about to take a turn**.
The climax is followed by a **resolution to the problem** and the story soon comes to an end.

Think about the climax in your story and what happened **just before** and **just after** that point.

Summarize the events just before, during, and just after the climax of your story.
Illustrate each section. Then write a short description of the action.

Just Before the Climax

The Climax

Just After the Climax